DATE DUE

Demco, Inc. 38-293

JUN 1 8 2009

May Swenson
Poetry Award Series

MRS. RAMSAY'S KNEE

poems
by

Idris Anderson

UTAH STATE UNIVERSITY PRESS
Logan, Utah

Utah State University Press
Logan, Utah 84322-7200
www.usu.edu/usupress

Cover design by Barbara Yale-Read
Cover art: Detail, "Touchstone: From the Sleeping Porch #2,"
  by Prilla Smith Brackett, 2004.
  http://prillasmithbrackett.com

Manufactured in the United States of America
Printed on recycled, acid-free paper

ISBN: 978-0-87421-718-6 (cloth)
ISBN: 978-0-87421-719-3 (paper)
ISBN: 978-0-87421-720-9 (e-book)

Library of Congress Cataloging-in-Publication Data

Anderson, Idris.
  Mrs. Ramsay's knee : poems / Idris Anderson.
     p. cm. -- (May Swenson Poetry Award series ; v. 12)
  ISBN 978-0-87421-718-6 (acid-free paper) -- ISBN 978-0-87421-719-3 (pbk. : acid-free
paper) -- ISBN 978-0-87421-720-9 (e-book)
  I. Title.
  PS3601.N5438M77 2008
  811'.6--dc22
                              2008008593

In memory of my parents

Dorothy Idris Hudson Baker
(1923–2003)

George Tyndall Baker
(1921–2002)

. . . for it was not knowledge
but unity that she desired,
not inscriptions on tablets,
nothing that could be written
in any language known to men,
but intimacy itself,
which is knowledge,
she had thought, leaning her head
on Mrs. Ramsay's knee.

Virginia Woolf
To the Lighthouse

CONTENTS

Acknowledgments   xi
Foreword   xiii

PROLOGUE
   Comet   3

RECOLLECTION OF TRANQUILITY

   The French Bed   7
   Recollection of Tranquility   8
   Bridges of Giverny   10
   Kehaya House   11
   Pumpkin Farm, Half Moon Bay   13
   Fugitive Effects   15
   The Temple of Poseidon   16
   Marsyas   18
   Fathers   21

FRONT PAGE *New York Times*   23

ROSES ON THE CEILING

   Dürer's Jerome   53
   Roses on the Ceiling   55
   Marble Boy   57
   Greek Stones   59
   Maiano   61
   Christine, Daughter of Immigrants   62
   The Moth   63
   The Bream   64
   Kayaks   66

Pretty Rooms

1. The Mower   71
2. Trio   71
3. Anniversary   72
4. Rousseau   72
5. At Night on the Terrace, Fiesole   73
6. Fourth of July   74
7. That Hat   74
8. The Turtle   75
9. Caravaggio   75
10. Conscience   76
11. Fig   76

The Red Coat

Lilies   79
On Throwing a Fish in the Well   80
Two at the Dock   82
Goat Song   83
The Red Coat   86
Above the Town   87
The Marsh   89
The Glider   92
No. 1   94
On a Bus to the Airport, Colorado   95

Epilogue
Face   97

Notes   99
About the Author   101
The May Swenson Poetry Award   102

ACKNOWLEDGMENTS

I would like to thank the editors of the following journals in which
the poems listed first appeared, sometimes in an earlier form:

The Hudson Review for "The French Bed" and "Dürer's Jerome"
The Nation for "The Bream"
Ontario Review for "Goat Song" and "Marble Boy"
The Paris Review for "Recollection of Tranquility"
Paris/Atlantic for "Christine, Daughter of Immigrants"
Southern Poetry Review for "Two at the Dock"
The Southern Review for "On Throwing a Fish in the Well"
ZYZZYVA for "Maiano" and "Pumpkin Farm, Half Moon Bay"

I am grateful to the faculty and staff of the MFA Program for
Writers at Warren Wilson College, especially Michael Collier,
Reginald Gibbons, Steve Orlen, and Alan Williamson. A sabbatical
semester from Crystal Springs Uplands School and fellowships from
the Vermont Studio Center, the Virginia Center for the Creative Arts,
and the Ragdale Foundation permitted me obligation-free time and
space for the completion of this book.

For reading and re-reading many of the poems and versions of
this manuscript and for helpful advice and encouragement, I owe
endless thanks: to Diane Harmon, most faithful reader; to my San
Francisco poetry group, Thirteen Ways, especially Robert Thomas;
to my Paris/New York e-group: Beverly Bie Brahic and Elizabeth
Haukaas. Also to Helen Vendler for teaching me to read; to Dean
Flower for opening doors; to Kathy Hill-Miller for a trip to the
lighthouse; to my students for their fresh, agile minds. I could not
have written this book without the great hearts and good listen-
ing ears of Peggy Cornelius, Marsha Irwin, Maureen Reinke, Mary
Stratton, Stephen Weislogel, Julie Ball, Terry Canizzaro, Louise
Aronson, Jane Langridge, and Carol Drowota (always). I owe most
to Suzanne Wilsey for daily pleasures: laughter, good cooking, and
conversations about *Othello* at five in the morning.

FOREWORD

The grave, measured poetic voice of Idris Anderson won me instantly, and repeated readings confirm the freshness of this remarkable poet. She has read deeply in Elizabeth Bishop, who I think would have liked this book. Anderson's mode is ekphrasis, on which the best guide is John Hollander's *The Gazer's Spirit*. The paintings by Rembrandt, Monet, Dürer, Balthus, Henri Rousseau, Jackson Pollock, and Chagall are among the very varied provocations that Anderson's gaze converts into poems. Elegant as her use of art works is, I am most taken by her stunning "Front Page," which reacts to *New York Times* photographs of the war between Israel and the Hezbollah in the summer of 2006.

Anderson is too compassionate to be detached, yet her tone is uncanny in these recent poems. She takes neither side but gives all to vividness. Where Bishop's art tended to be on the threshold between the visual and the visionary, Anderson's swerve from her great precursor adheres to the visual, and yet teases from it what can be seen as an intimation at once immanent and transcendental.

Whether Anderson relies too much on painting and photographs will be more of a question when she goes on to a second book. Bishop's famous eye was too much emphasized; we can judge now that her angle of vision counts for more than her descriptive precision. Anderson, like Bishop, tacitly undoes all ideologies.

This book's epigraph, from Virginia Woolf's *To the Lighthouse*, gives us the provenance of her title. She seeks "intimacy itself, which is knowledge, she had thought, leaning her head on Mrs. Ramsay's knee." At their best, Anderson's poems seek an intimacy with the reader, but never by way of confession, which I have trouble accepting in Robert Lowell.

It is difficult to prophesy Anderson's future development, partly because her poems until now are mostly consonant with one author. It may be that, again like Bishop, her poetry will unfold rather than change. Still, the single poem I like best in her first book is the beautiful reverie on the death of John Keats, where a new tonality emerges:

> We want to be changed
> by what we enter, the dry,
> bright air of warmer places
> to which we book passage,

roads of emperors and poets strewn
with marble victories,
intimate rooms where the famous
dead lived vividly, where what
was beautiful was not easy
and what was true was almost endurable.

The intricate cognitive music of that stanza is heard more intently, because Anderson has no design upon us. Very subtly she plays upon the message that ends the "Ode on a Grecian Urn," where "beauty is truth, truth beauty" is an absolute gesture. To know that the beautiful is difficult and that the truth is "almost endurable" is not a correction of Keats but a tribute to the pathos of his death. As with Shelley and Hart Crane, our loss was enormous. That sense of bereavement is expressed admirably by Anderson's hushed eloquence.

Harold Bloom

MRS. RAMSAY'S KNEE

Prologue

COMET

The comet doesn't come as promised in that portion
of the sky; our binoculars aren't good enough
for searching planets; we know it's pointless

to count stars. Making jokes about fools
not dead yet, we lie back in the scorched
suburban grass, breathing the cooling dew,

the full effect of sky, so many stars.
I wish I knew the names of constellations
or could find for you Orion, stalking our summer.

No moon is out, no clouds to help us feel
the earth move; crickets sing the only music
of the spheres, as idle, with nothing to speak of, we wait—

for deeds that we have done and left undone,
and which are these and how are we to know?—
some consequence yet hanging in the stars.

RECOLLECTION
OF TRANQUILTY

THE FRENCH BED

I can't speak from the man's point of view,
but as a woman, I'd say this etching tells truth
about sex. The lover is kneeling for his own pleasure
first, then hers too, perhaps. His foot is flexed
for pushing energetically. He's as deep
as he can go into the soft folds of her flesh.
And she, with knees frankly spread, is telling him
with fingers where and how he should move.
Notice the eyes, they are so wise with each other.
It's not a brothel. He was in love with this wife.

Rembrandt, in his exuberance, gave the girl
three arms. One hand we see stroking the side
of her lover's back, another reaches round for his bum,
and the third, a fully visible limb, lies limp
on the bed, as if she's totally compliant, or done.
The bed is well made, with canopy and draperies,
the linens as plush as her thighs. She's relaxed into what
he desires; she's eager and wants her own pleasure too.
The drypoint's velvety strokes so accurate. He saw
what he wanted and made it, and wanted what he saw.

After all the crosses, Christs feeding the peasants,
rooftops and ruins, beggars in hats, here is
domestic interior—fine inked-up lines swirled
into rumpled bedclothes and bodies' vulnerable
curlings—her sweet face, his competent shoulders.
A scribbling style, tender and swift, all gesture
and touch. The needle's hard burr softens and makes
vivid the intimacy, the inwardness, the mutual desire.
What comes after seduction, the drapery drawn
for our eyes—what we want desperately is this.

The first time we ever quarreled
you were cutting an onion
in the kitchen of our rented cottage.
I remember vividly. We were making creole
for a late night supper with champagne,
and you were taking it seemed forever
to cut the onion.
Each time your dull paring knife
chopped on the counter, I shifted my feet,
and I saw once in a glimpse over my shoulder
a white wedge of onion wobbling loose.
I sighed inaudibly. The butter I stirred
had already bubbled and browned.
I was starting over with a new yellow lump
that was slipping on the silver aluminum
when you brought, cupped in your hands,
the broken pieces, the edges all ragged,
the layers separated, bruised and oozing
cloudy white onion juice.
I complained:
the family recipe stated specifically,
the onion must be "finely chopped,"
for what I explained were very good reasons.
Otherwise, the pungent flavors would be trapped
irrevocably in the collapsed cellular structure
of the delicate root.

You sighed, I guess, inaudibly
and adjusted your glasses carefully
with two fingers (a fidget
I have since come to know
as a sign of mild perturbation)
and explained:
the pungence of onions too finely chopped
would be simmered away. The original sharp

burning crispness could be retained
only in fairly large, bite-sized chunks.
But you wouldn't fight tradition.
I chopped onion on the counter
with the dull knife, while you set the table
and figured the best way of popping the cork.

BRIDGES OF GIVERNY

Creosote pilings of my father's dock
are encrusted too with barnacles that sputter
bubbles of the green marsh at low tide;
the salt river laps and feeds

those living accretions lavishly:
they smell like oysters
and keep themselves open
for whatever comes.

When you write "encrusted"
on a picture postcard from Boston,
I see a pond piled thick
with Monet's jeweled colors.

Blue-brushed white lilies float under
the bridges, encrusted with paints
of morning lights, red shadows
of a day dying in the garden.

"Ugly, muddy," you write, but when
you walk away and look back from light
of real trees in a real garden, a window
in the room where the paintings are hung,

clouds shift in the dark glimmering waters —
illusions of motion, this seeing
and making, holiest of mysteries,
the fully encrusted mind.

I write here by a blue light of sky
in California. The hills are golden.
I can see the Bay and the Carolina
dock as surely as you've seen

the Japanese bridges, the muddy
blues and greens of aqueous light—
pictures between us, cities,
even whole continents.

KEHAYA HOUSE

I had no mind for winter when I arrived
and saw the snow outside and entered the house
where you lived in the heaviest coat I owned
and borrowed gloves
                              and stamped ice from my boots
inside your kitchen door. January, New England.
Already dark or near dark
                              yet I remember that first
moving into as shadowless, noon-lit.

Blue-patterned plates from Old City, Jerusalem
propped in your Irish-pine hutch.

I thought I'd known you in another life,
that first summer. Talk
                              over menus before *Othello*
in Santa Cruz. The waiter kept returning.

Copper pots from Italy. A cluster of houses from Camogli
on the coast of Liguria.
                              From the kitchen ceiling.
On the mantel in the living room.
Cities you've lived in, objects of your world.

What we had said then and what we had done.
Tickets. Seats. Intermission.
                              The long late drive
to where I lived, north through mountains.

Animals roamed every surface: olivewood camel,
ceramic rhinoceros, soapstone elephants, ebony hippo.
Zambia, Kenya.
                    A trooping of antelopes
carved in a curve of pale Nairobian wood.

Up the coast on a narrow black road, *Desdemona's skin
whiter is than snow*
                              and smooth as monumental alabaster.

I was quoting everything I know by heart,

                              how he'd won her
with stories of dangers he had passed.

A painting in your dining room "Turkey Pond in Snow"
of water and shadows and cold.

                    And "Mumble" a big-lit
square on your bedroom wall: children in a ringed
conspiracy of faces,

                    their shoes, their rumpled clothes,
the boy with his hands pushed in his back pockets.

Put out the light, and then put out the light.

Accidents. Betrayals. A weapon in a pool.
A handkerchief dropped.

                    . . . there's magic in the web of it.
How far would one go to keep what is loved?
Her pillow. His smothering kiss.

                         Some things yellow.
Some things, like stories in a bottle, unfold and endure.

Everything you owned packed up and moved across a continent.

Above our kitchen sink "Leaf," a slight
gold thing unfurling—could paint be
so transparent, I thought then?—

                         a delicacy you couldn't resist
when you saw it. In Milan, was it?

                         or Florence?
You imagined washing dishes looking at this.
Beauty so every-day, ordinary.

Looking out again in the snowy wood, a bright glare
in the just-dark,

                    I'd thought of daffodils you'd planted
in the fallen leaves, two hundred hard, secret knots.

PUMPKIN FARM, HALF MOON BAY

Now you veer away from me like a sailor on his keel
into a windless place, into gold corn blades coiling
in the dry light-and-shade of furrows run over everywhere
with vines, brown curls rasping like metal files
against the cotton weave of your sweatshirt.
You enter the rows shoulder first, sideways.
A note I make of your character: that instinct
to minimize destruction, whistling the scalpel's
shining lyric all the way into a dark veiny passage,
stitching the wound to stop the pain.
Meanwhile a crowd of schoolchildren out of school
managed only loosely by their teachers
are bruising the natural world, their voices
high-pitched confusions of sea birds. Clumps
of little boys and girls climbing blocks of hay,
piles of pumpkins, the big green tractor.
They are everywhere, a scramble of jostlings
and tumblings, the flinging of arms as they jump,
the pumping of fists into shoulders. I know
the changing expressions of the faces
and what is likely to happen next: boys lift
pumpkins the size of basketballs over their heads,
trying to smash them, wanting to see them explode.
You turn back to say something I'm too far away to hear.
The trouble with me is I worry too much about intrusion,
and imagine too purely someone else's passions
and get them wrong. Some days everything seems
pointless. What moves any of us to do what we do?
I go around the field of corn on a rutted
tractor road, pushing a barrow of pumpkins to the car.
And you? Whatever you've said is over.
You're seeing between the rows the same unruly
mess of tissues, organs, shapes
such as those you've learned to cut into,
cutting like Aeneas through waves blown red and black

by a cold wind, one city or another at his back
burning, and nothing in the way of his future.
In the offing there is nothing but blue, water and sky—
the straight, the narrow, the exact.
In your mind you're rehearsing some procedure—
the yards, the riggings, the sutures yare in your hands.
This, like this. Yes, yes. This. You're seeing
what in the body is in the way, occlusions and clamps
and the new sealing knife that burns the bleeders shut.

FUGITIVE EFFECTS

A voice behind me speaks: *Don't move.*
Stay there, says the voice again,
and I turn to see a stranger settling
on a bench in front of the pictures. Open face.
Shopping bags from Marshall Fields.
It's the color, she says. *Don't move.*
I'm wearing a shirt saturated with blue,
like the blue in the haystacks. What is this
instant intimacy with strangers?
Her eyes catch blue.

Geometry of haystacks on the wall,
old mutual friends. Blur of snow effect.
Monet left not a trace of the easel he dragged
across stubble fields of brown and blue.
Compositions shift. Autumn evening strikes
a tinge of red in the straw. Physics of light.
Fugitive effects. Is that what he wrote,
what he knew, and why I come?

She's a designer of kitchens, it turns out,
and likes looking at things done over and over—
pieces fitted together, newly arranged.
Grammar of umber, vowel of cerulean blue.
We are catching up on what is going on
in the world, relieved to be here.

I consider the houses among the trees.
Rooftops, I'd never noticed, just discernible
in strokes of coppery blue. So tiny. Just suggestions.
And the woman who saw me
as part of the landscape—
when I turn around again, she's gone.

THE TEMPLE OF POSEIDON

1

In the shadow of the Temple of Poseidon I swam once
in the salty Mediterranean, slants of sharp light streaming
through columns where Byron cut his name, back-lit
in the morning glare. I swam, floated rather—
the water buoyant with salt—paddled out to where
I could see ancient boat slips, long V-shaped gouges
carved in bottom rock so far under water
you wouldn't see them unless someone told you
where to look, an ancient harbor for epic black ships.

The Temple of Poseidon is so high up on rock so far out
on Point Sunion, you look up to it when you swim
like an ordinary human below it, and you wonder
if the god of the sea, of the world—still dark,
changeable, uncertain—if the great god
was propitiated, even temporarily, by such labor
and beauty, such an architectural feat,
not to stir up angry waters with his great oar.

Or did Poseidon himself, when the Temple was newly
completed, have a sense of humor, call a party of the gods
to celebrate, to wallow around on their backs in these waters,
old salty boys having fun, letting their hair go?
He could wave his trident and make the waters dance
like horses, could make the full-cheeked clouds blow
and fill the pretty sails of pleasure boats.
He would speed around the harbor, watching
the candle of the sky light his birthday cake.

2

There is still a little harbor, some small boats on buoys,
and a shack with good fried-up baby kalamari.
I was looking forward to eating lunch there,

the Greek fisherman-cook, his rope-carved hands.
Until the sun was too hot I swam around thinking
about gods and warriors, how remote they are.
When salt crusted on my shoulders, I thought of Odysseus,
his long swim after shipwreck, his hair matted like seaweed,
his shoulders crusted with salt. Odysseus, who had the wit
in such a condition, naked, cut-up, to speak to the beautiful
Nausikaa, who stood tall and unafraid near the washing pools,
the colorful laundry drying on the rocks. Her friends
had fled up the hillside at the sight of the beast.

She had a mind of her own
and knew what he was when he spoke.

The story is essentially about cleanness,
the shaking out of salt, preparing oneself for a stranger
who is noble and instantly beloved.
And thus in spite of ugliness and exhaustion–
the brine flakes on his shoulders as thick as fish scales
he would scrub off in the river's mouth and emerge clean
in new clothes the young girl had given him—
he defeated his enemy Poseidon, old maker of shipwrecks.
He had a rare voice, a civilized nerve
to approach beauty, without complaint or apology,
and to win the heart.

3

Everything here is intense, boiled down, concentrated,
dried up to salt and rock and the fluctuating waters
of myth and history. Poets have been drawn to this place
and men who need war and men who need gods.
And here, in an easy life, was I once, a traveler. I came
for the view and the history, the swim and the tender kalamari.

MARSYAS

In such cavernous public spaces as the Pantheon
      and St. Paul's, citizens of the world have congregated
And cut deals, passed grimy, imperial coins, dope,
      envelopes, poems of blackmail and seduction,
And love of course. Behind a column in a corner
      slipped a stiff penis in a dress.
Here a gentleman came to find an easy
      stroller, of one sex or another, the sacred
Notwithstanding: marble gods in gilded niches,
      gaudily painted, a martyr on a cross,
High arched windows shooting ruby and blue.
      Here all hours of the day a market of exchanges,
Whisperings and muffled laughter, good gossip,
      good jokes, good business too sometimes, sometimes
A stolen prayer going up in choking smoke.

I think of the traffic of such places as we cross the Thames
      in light winter rain, tilting our colored umbrellas
Over our ignoble desires. We want our glut
      of art raw, expressive, massive, modern.
The Tate. This cold box of glass, concrete,
      steel, an empty turbine hall so big
It could hold—how many, did they say?—
      double-decker London buses stacked
Seven high. Inside the gutted power plant,
      we're ingested by a flower, as if by Georgia
O'Keeffe, though large, elongated, trumpet-headed,
      red bell of the flute Athena cast aside:
It made her ugly when she puffed her cheeks and blew.

"I want to turn earth into sky,"
      the metaphysician proposed grandiosely
To some committee and won the prize. Sculptor,
      turned geometrician, he calculated, and so
Flesh flies, industrialized, the wine-red
      PVC membrane stitched and stretched

From ring to ring to ring. We feel, just walking in,
        devoured. Do Not Touch, says the sign,
But we want to, this flesh, too tender. It pulls one apart
        from another. When you walk away and say nothing,
I want to know what you mean, your head drawn back
        like Eurydice, both of us wanting to touch, to see
The skin of Marsyas. You don't. And neither do I.

Clearly we have to keep moving to locate meaning.
        We climb to the middle of the bridge under another
Red round mouth of the flower which blooms yet again
        at the far east end of the hall. We can't see
What it is all at once, but can see what it is at last:
        In a cave near Calaenae in Phrygia, Apollo flayed
The skin of Marsyas, who'd dared the pitiless god
        with the pretty music of his flute and lost unfairly.
Later, in grief, Apollo cut strings from his lyre,
        the satyr's blood became the river Marsyas.
His bleeding here, though large, is under control.

I'm thinking of war, how this too was one
        of the bombed-out places, how it begins every time
Innocently enough with a contest; how even the gods
        and angels do it to themselves—the bigger, the better,
The more beautiful—a victor every time and the death of one.
        Engines without pity gone now, a residual roaring,
Voices of aficionados indistinguishable from our own voices,
        from the cries of babies and the whines of tourists.
A lull of peace, intimations of a war to come—
   ·   I've seen the headlines on the newsstands
In the underground: we cannot escape the world.

Whatever we mean, make, or are is abstract,
        abstracted—yanked out of myth or history,
Out of Plato's cave or Titian's vision of Marsyas.
        Later, on the other side of the river, I saw again
The anxious ghost in that portrait of Iris Murdoch,
        a piece of Titian's painting painted behind

Her matter-of-fact, unstylish, banged, frank face.
    What had she lived through that she would know
A language for all our little immoralities?

A smear of blood. A flap of skin that wouldn't
    heal on my mother's leg. A red hole to
White bone. Now in old age she remembers
    the man who left her in the time of war,
And not because he was a hero. He wasn't.
    In the battle of the Bulge he was, that flood of blood,
And came back, all right, but not to her. How naïve
    she was, my sweet mother, tiny and beautiful,
And too much in love even then not to trust.
    And this is the way I am trying to understand
The exuberance of Marsyas, his infatuation
    with music and the consequence of passion.
How naïve he was, we all are, when we're
    in love and choose the life we enter, as we must,
As I do here with you, examining his skin.

Now by the Thames in a gloom of late light,
    by the barges and the bridges and the empty offices,
The glittering, misty lights come on the muddy tidal river.
    We walk, we talk, we haven't much to say, except—
The dome of St. Paul's, you notice, is softly lit,
    and to the east, I see, the orange metal crisscross
Of a crane perfectly vertical on the black sky.   .
    Marsyas, I'm thinking, Marsyas—what instruments we use
To cut out a space for ourselves in a difficult world.
    Some terrors we've heard and can predict,
Some magic in the music and the shapes we still must make.

FATHERS

1. ICEPICKS

Cleaning out your father's tool shed we discover his meat hooks
in wood boxes among broken saw blades, the empty arc of a hacksaw,
huge ice-tongs you remember (blue blocks of ice hauled in
every morning), dull icepicks so large we can't figure what they are
until you remember his white shirt and taut shoulders, the white nails
of his clenched hand like Abraham's, the ritual jabbing and chipping
clean ice for the cases. You grew up spoiled by red beefsteaks
piled from the freezers, barrels of red snapper steaks,
white fish flesh beautiful as egret feathers—meat cut so deftly
the place was practically bloodless, the ice underneath always edible.
And so they are icepicks, rusting in the humid heat of this city.
We detect no bloodstains on wood handles, not even a thumbprint.
White enameled meat trays hang on nails over our heads.
You remember eating icicles in midsummer.

2. NIGHT SHIFT

Into your eight-hour, day-night shift of tracks,
railyard, private world of steel, I come
among slow rumbling loads of moving cars.
I know where you are. Weak station lights diffuse.
Fifty yards into the void, your face is fixed,
impassive under that billed hat. You contemplate cargo:
trains of sugar to New York, grain to Florida.
Inside the lantern's circled light, you walk the track,
swinging glare scattered starward. Listen, if you cannot see:
the switchman's shout, the distant clang of coupling
cars, the jolt, the hiss of brakes released.
Your heavy shoes crunch gravel, kick a loose tie.
You wait. Slowly up and down, your lantern moves,
a clear signal I never understood.

FRONT PAGE
NEW YORK TIMES

Let the atrocious images haunt us.

Susan Sontag
Regarding the Pain of Others

THURSDAY, JULY 13, 2006
—*photo by Oded Balilty*

Artillery battery and a tank. Fire power
of war in colors and shapes,
pallets of munitions, tarps

scattered on slopes of summer dry grass.
We look for what is human here.
Soldiers crouch and cover their ears

against the blast, small dark bodies
curled on the tank, on the ground
behind the tank. One tends a stash

of rockets up-ended like sharpened
pencils on their erasers. Others
break open crates, feed machinery.

Fire of charge and double-charge
lights up a white mass of cloud.
Composition with blue and white

flag, high in the bright, burnt air.
Of all the photographs of the first day
of war, an editor chose this one

to fill the space above the fold
under a terribly familiar headline.
Retaliations. Recriminations.

What has been done to us we must
do to others. It's the blood we obey.
We who watch are in awe

of the wreck of the world,
destruction's beauty, its litter and smoke,
a beauty that tells us who we are.

FRIDAY, JULY 14, 2006

—photo by Adnan Hajj

Airport fuel tanks burn sun-orange
above the night city, a fire that will not
go out. A plane in the dark foreground

is stuck on the tarmac, a spot of gleam
on its landing gear, a thin, short streak
at the end of its fuselage.

Up the hillside thousands of small lights
like stars. The windows of Beirut
where invisible people look out

on blackness, coldness, stillness, and the furious
fire. They hold no candle to the fire.
There's no way to fly out of here.

Home safe somewhere else, I look through
a window and count my neighbors' lights.

SATURDAY, JULY 15, 2006
—photo by Pierre Boukaren

A soldier is standing where a building was,
at the edge of a crater full of dirty water,
sewage perhaps, even likely, structure
and infrastructure bombed out.

What's left of the building in the background
is reflected in orange-brown water, the grace
of its curve around the corner, the architecture
of its blue windows and doors,

the colors of signage high on the building
clean-bright, the advertisements of a modern city.
We can't smell anything and so the picture
is aesthetically pleasing. We'd say,

he has a good eye for telling a story.
In the distance are people so small there are no
expressions on their faces. But the soldier with his back
to the crater has pressed the fingers of his hands

in the edges of his hair, his head tilts,
his knees bend weakly, his rifle droops
at his waist, the barrel of it pointed down
at a patch of shattered glass.

SUNDAY, JULY 16, 2006

—photo by Hassan Ammar

Three body bags are blue,
    unzipped, the flaps turned back
from faces. Eight more
tumbled roughly in blankets
    and black rubber sheets.

Five of sixteen are missing,
    already claimed or unsorted
pieces out of the picture.
The bags lie on squares
    of clear plastic sheets

on the concrete street
    of the make-shift morgue,
squares that grow smaller,
more infinite, the deeper
    I look in the picture.

On the curb of the street,
    forty or fifty people stand and wait
for what's now to be done.
Arms folded, hands in pockets,
    they don't look at each other.

In the center of the picture,
    a man in a white mask walks
between the bodies, toward
the camera. He looks for
    color of skin,

breath, movement of a finger,
   a wound that bleeds. He wears
green camouflage clothes,
his hands in white
   rubber gloves

level with his shoulders,
   like a surgeon who's
scrubbed up and doesn't
   want to touch
anything that is foul.

MONDAY, JULY 17, 2006

—photo by Oded Balilty

Red diagonal lines of the station platforms
rake dramatically down from the top left
corner of the picture and make whatever
has happened here seem inevitable.
The rails are heavy with speed,
mechanical and black.

Bottom right corner,
there's so much more light,
the figures larger, irregular, busy
with gesture. Emergency vests a neon
yellow, hard helmets a bright school-bus
yellow, black yarmulkes, Hasidic beards.

The body on the gurney is strapped neatly in
at the waist. Red strap around the bag,
a glare of bright white with official
blue insignia. I count
seventeen workers

carefully focused
on recovery of the victim,
of missile strikes on this train station.
If I focus, can I feel the feelings of others?
Is it moral to observe pain? Can I be moved

by adjective and adverb, when noun and verb
are the cries of somebody else? Slamming,
damning questions speed toward me
like my father's trains, no lights
sweeping the tracks.

TUESDAY, JULY 18, 2006
—*photo by Tyler Hicks*

Two men weep in a bomb's crater, a clay pit,
the ground where they sit gouged in rough shapes,
irregular slopes and cracks, some roots of pipes.

Old earth turned up is new again, the same fresh
orange-red earth ancient peoples used to make mud brick.
The modern recipe's nearly the same. War is the same.

The men are exhausted, their shoulders fallen, their wet
trousers and shirts splattered with clay. One pushes
his forehead into the older man's back, the wild, spent

energy of grief, his arm around his neck.
                              When the bomb dropped,
three children were swimming in an irrigation ditch,
their bodies recovered, just out of the picture.

The younger man holds his smeared glasses.
In the fingers of the older man, a cigarette burns.

SATURDAY, JULY 22, 2006

—photo by Tyler Hicks

It's all about mathematics and geometry, these deaths,
these dead piling up. What's to be done
with the bodies until, when the bombing stops,
funerals are safe?

Here's a system for you: plywood fence painted white,
a row of big black numbers spray-painted on:
25, 26, 27, 28, 29, 30, 31, 32, 33, 34—

Here are coffins, trapezoids, bigger at the top
for the width of shoulders and chests,
one below each number.

Someone has scrawled Arabic script on each lid
in red or black: name, identification, location, date?
You wonder, are they color-coded?

Each coffin is shorter or longer, depending . . . well, you know.

Number 29 is the shortest, maybe three, three-and-a-half feet.

A long, heavy one is coming in on the shoulders
of two young men, Giacometti-thin,
one taller than the other. Their long strides
and the sharp shadow of a leg under their feet
construct perfect triangles, equilateral.

86 coffins in total, we are told, but you can't see
the whole picture in the picture.
No one could capture the whole.
So you hunt for an angle, a certain slant
of clean light, a rectangular shape,
and fit what you can in.

SUNDAY, JULY 23, 2006

—photo by João Silva

Four white plastic chairs on the pier
look comfortable for reading, or drying off
in the sun after a swim. There is sun and that Mediterranean
    blue in the sky.

High on the skyline, smoke blows black and then gray
as it spreads like contagion, over beaches and boat slips,
over high-rise hotels, from left to right
    like a train across the picture.

The chairs are clustered in no particular arrangement.
An umbrella closed down on a stand by itself. The pier is roped off.
Plastic floats in primary colors square
    a neat area for swimming.

But no one is swimming or reading a book or sucking
something sweet from a straw. It's a resort but no one is here.
There are ghosts, but no one sees them. Even the lady in the harbor,
    who lifts her hands to welcome ships,

cannot see them. She looks Greek, the stone folds of her drapery
carved classically. She bends a knee, as if she's walking
steadily on water. She refuses to look
    at the smoke at her back.

MONDAY, JULY 24, 2006

—*photo by Tyler Hicks*

To be in the right place at the wrong time
where disaster is brutal, the burned face,
the burned eyes of the adolescent boy—
how do you do it, Tyler Hicks?
What instinct, what cunning
puts you within feet of the boy?

In the hospital parking lot at Tirens,
the boy is rigid in the arms of his father,
whose body, urgent and needy,
wants his son whole again.
You can see it in his face, in the quick,
deep breath of his mouth,
in his knees pushing the weight
of the boy. Out of panic he wrenches
a difficult determination.
He leans into time.

Somehow you are aware of a script
of doors. The father's eye fixed
on the hospital door. And that apparently useless
detail in the background:
the car door left open.
You are aware of emergency, of emotions
that come out from within.
The heavy mother, kerchiefed, in black clothes,
has her hand on her son. In the wind of the rush,
her black coat opens, flowing with the speed.

But you, Tyler Hicks, I'm asking,
when the shutter clicked open,
was passion or dispassion the cue
for this picture, this miracle of focus,
except for the blur of the boy's
rapidly moving fist, like a bird?

The image we have: of Hecuba, Medea. We don't
believe her, dismiss her, assume this is performance
for the stage or the camera.
                           Grief should go quietly
inward, get to a nunnery. Or in silence off stage,
she should hang herself, drown herself, eat hot coals.

The woman in Haifa is hysterical. Look at her, can I,
and not turn the page?
                           High in one hand she holds
a photograph of her brother, who's dead. She knows

it's over. Three women sit behind her, patient,
waiting for news. The oldest looks at her: she's gone
mad; she's tearing her hair. It's classic, this grief.

Look again, can I? Yellow dress with blue flowers.
That sound in the throat.
                           Can I weep for her?
                                      A photograph.
Four women in Haifa against a concrete block wall.

WEDNESDAY, JULY 26, 2006

—photo by Kai Pfaffenbach

It's victory or gloat—
depending on your point of view.

Three soldiers ride high
in an armoured personnel carrier,
the camera angle from below.

One stretches his arms like a Christ
to display the trophy: a red and white
Lebanese flag, with a green cedar tree,
the sign of victory in his fingers.

The Hezbollah flag is sideways and backwards.
Yellow and green, a green gun held up by a green hand.
A big ripped hole. The slogan in Arabic script from the Quran:
Then surely the party of Allah are they that shall be triumphant.

They look bloated in thick flak jackets, body-stuffed
like scarecrows, pockets bulging, hard helmets molded
extra wide at the ears for headphones, microphones bent
around to their mouths. Can they hear
anything but the noise of machinery?

Three Israeli boys mugging the camera.

FRIDAY, JULY 28, 2006
—photo by Lynsey Addario

They carry their guns to the funeral.
Green combat uniforms, red berets.
One holds his face in his hands.

Others look down at the grave
the angle of the camera does not
permit us to see.

Seven fragments of faces. Planes
of light, clean-shaven. Jaws set
against grief.

Soldiers. Highly trained
and young. One nudges forward
with the blue, bright metal of his gun.

A baby, still beautiful
in the arms of her father,
who stands by the grave

where he will lay her, cover her,
a clay box we see chiseled
in the sun-hard dirt, a red

hole just large enough
to hold her. Hands reach in
from edges of the photograph, palms up—

the instinct of neighbors
when no God is listening
and what can be done may be done

only for the father whose strength
comes like a miracle
from his hands. He bends

to the open face of his daughter,
her small body loosely wound
in fabric generously

folded and tied with white ribbons
above and below the face,
at the waist, at the feet,

the cotton smooth-white,
whiter than newsprint.

The paratroopers are singing as they march
briskly from the battle. It's over. The drop.
The skirmish. The scramble back through live
fire. Adrenaline still surging, they carry

a wounded comrade level on their shoulders.
Ten, fifteen of them. It's easy. So many arms
to hold him shoulder high, feet forward,
his leg strapped with white. No blood.

There's a rhythm, the crunch of their boots
in the cracked earth. They are dirty, hungry.
They kick up dust. Their mouths open.
Heat in their bodies. Air in their chests.

Some are grinning. All are singing.
Adam's apples ripe in their necks.

TUESDAY, AUGUST 1, 2006

—photo by Tyler Hicks

She's brought out of rubble
on a sheet from her bed,
too broken to walk,

her head on a pillow printed with flowers,
kerchief knot at her throat.
A grandmother, anyone's.

I try to see, then to think:
impossible to act or to feel.
She reaches out in a gesture I don't know

how to read. Her eyes, squint
in the sun, don't plead so much as
command; mouth open

as if to speak or breathe.
It must be hard to breathe,
the dust and the stench.

She hid in a bathroom, then a basement,
a storeroom full of yarn, ate pieces of bread
and grain from her cupboard, lost track of time.

In the calm between airstrikes, strangers
haul her out from the ruin.
A hand in a plastic glove reaches

for her hand. A man in a green surgical
mask looks at the camera.
On the face of another I read:

it wasn't easy to get here, the roads blocked,
the blockade in the harbor, the bombs
still falling after a ceasefire.

In the background, the blasted block houses—
walls broken, roofs collapsed.
Nearby, another woman in a kerchief bends

into shadow near the old woman's face.
Sister, friend, neighbor? Whoever you are,
I don't need to read the cutline below

to learn whose side you are on, what
village is yours, what country, what world.
The camera has composed the perfect shot.

FRIDAY, AUGUST 4, 2006

—photo by Yonathan Weitzman

They look down at blood on the floor,
splattered and smeared like fingerpaint
on a tile-block grid. She carries on her hip

a boy, two or three years old. She's caught
by the hand a girl, four or five, and steers her
to the side of the largest pool.

She's not wearing shoes but seems not to worry
about glass. Nothing's broken. The walls are washed
in hot afternoon light, yellow and pink.

Her face is intent, her whole body in a posture
we know: instinct, speed. It's a kitchen
or a hallway from a kitchen—cabinets, doors.

Bright gray angular splashes—bombed out
floors of a concrete building exposed, the edges
of color muted, blurred. And below,
billows of cloud, friable smoke-dust debris
dispersed like fog. A stain painting
or water color abstraction, like landscapes I know
by Helen Frankenthaler. I study its geometry
and make out the black-scissor legs of a man
clinging to a jagged wall, the blue-gray shirt
of another on a ladder or ledge. It's hard to see
what's happening, but beautiful to look at.
I want it to be beautiful and a little something
astonishing to please me—the mauve-pink
light of reflected fire from somewhere.

WEDNESDAY, AUGUST 9, 2006

—photo by James Hill

Street scene in Damascus. Split frame,
inside and outside. In the café
a man smokes at a table under the TV.
A couple we see from the back look up
at the man with a tie on the Hezbollah station.
She with long pulled-back hair, he
with a bald spot. They listen intensely.
Reports and reactions. Elbows, nerves. We can't see
what they've eaten, if it's coffee they drink.

The TV floats over a wall of polished
blond wood carved in shallow relief: hands up
to Allah, a sacred text held by a man
in a chair, and a muscular figure bent
to a child, forehead to forehead. Allegories,
prayers, quiet personal conspiracies.

A plant that is green in the corner.

Outside two men on the neat brick
sidewalk gesticulate, unaware of
the camera. The man with the gray
beard, gray suit, smart knotted tie,
talks to the man in a blue open-neck shirt.
They walk by the plate-glass window
that splits the scene. A complicated
exposure. The café is too bright. The electric
lamps stream like fire up the street.

The talk, inside and out, is the same.

THURSDAY, AUGUST 10, 2006
—photo by Addul-Ahad

They've rolled into the river
pieces of a broken concrete culvert
and something that looks like a petrified tree.
The last link over rushing white water,
a red stretcher, set from rock to rock.

Three Red Cross workers, two wounded
fighters. They step gingerly on the make-shift
bridge over the Litani. It's not easy.
Everything wobbles.

Red suits, white hard hats with red crosses.
One fighter, his back to the camera,
walks on bare feet. The other limps,
his foot in a sandal, his knee bandaged.
He's holding a white business-sized envelope
between his face and the camera, the black hood
of the Hezbollah fighter over his head.

Bridges blown out.
No way out, and no way in.
Except by furtive, make-shift
causes and causeways.

SUNDAY, AUGUST 13, 2006

—photo by John Moore

They have marched over the hill, following a road
into a valley, toward the river, and a village.
The road winds in that S-shape photographers

love—for its picturesque grace, its definition
of deep space. The soldiers are strung out
along the road, and though they are loaded down

with gear, and their green camouflage clothes are hot,
they walk in clusters of friends, fool around a little,
slap shoulders, tell jokes. They carry their weapons

haphazardly. It's a hike. It's a lovely morning.
The village in the distance is the color of the sandy road,
the color of the wild weeds and thistles on the hillside.

The thistles, already bloomed, are large dry balls of sharp
needle-thorns. Seven miles north of the border, two miles
from the river. An enemy in each house in the village.

TUESDAY, AUGUST 15, 2006

—photo by Lynsey Addario

Little girl, you have kept your doll close,
though the building is broken, the floors
slid down the slope of the street,
the dust still rising.

The camera is tilted so nothing
squares up. It's disorienting, hard
to know if you're standing on flat ground.
You've turned to look down the street.

There's a ghost—someone at first
I don't see—the top of her face
just visible above the head of your doll.

The ghost is your mother whose silk
sleeve pulls you tight. She's shy
of the camera and hides behind you.

———

The woman holding the camera
is not visible at all. She's a professional.
She's erased herself, even as she views
through a lens this picture I look at.

The hands of your mother I see now,
clinched in a fireman's hold. You're
too big to carry, she carries you
anyway, her mouth near your ear.

I take pleasure in the bright green
of your little girl skirt, the bright pink
swoop of your mother's embrace.

I hold a coffee cup level, steady
in my hand and tilt the corner
of the page to eliminate glare.

WEDNESDAY, AUGUST 16, 2006
—photo by Tyler Hicks

Night black. The bombing's stopped.
Ink saturates the dry matte newsprint,
   almost the whole upper half
of the page, a black house wall.

Lower left: a square of glow
from candles in their hands, an open
   door. The man and wife have stopped
a little way into their house and look

on nothing particular, a vacancy, the bombed out
interior in their metaphysical eyes.
   What they have lived through—
the rage, the reasons, even the history

of their fathers' fathers—is what
they know and have known again,
   this still inexplicable moment
of shame they have come home to.

Nothing surprises. Nothing within them can ever
completely break. Over her head, a clean white
   scarf she has folded and wound
around her neck and shoulders.

The solid fact of his standing near her.
He looks through the door. The shutter opens
   and closes. It's a portrait. Witness to a time
they will again and again obey.

Upper right: a large irregular hole,
like a puzzle piece punched through the wall—
   the same interior orange-pink glow,
which I mistook at first for sky.

FRIDAY, SEPTEMBER 1, 2006
—photo by Dimitri Messinis

In Ouzai, south of Beirut, open trucks move war rubble.
I count forty or more on three lanes of a wide highway
curving by the sea. New trucks. Bumper to bumper, they wait

for a turn at the dump ahead. A finger of new ground grows
as the power shovel drops its load, flattening, rearranging
the landscape. A billboard on the beach advertises

a vacation spot. It looks like the coast of Normandy:
large arched rugged rocks in a sea the color of this sea.
A billboard band of white sky merges with a fringe

of actual breaking waves. Photograph within photograph.
Inside the curve of trucks, a geometry of side panels:
parallelograms yellow and orange and blue. In the nearest ones,

concrete chunks and cables frayed, twisted pipes.
Each truck must have a driver, whose radio's on—to music or news.
Each driver must see the billboard and the giant shovel's empty maw.

ROSES ON THE CEILING

DÜRER'S JEROME

The saint, before he is a saint, is comfortably at work in a room
like one of Dürer's own in his fine house in Nuremberg.
Sun streams through windows. It's warm. The dozy lion blinks.
Jerome is pouring out his eyes on a holy text that is brittle,
that is already crumbling into dust, already burning.
His dry pen scratches down the cold meaning of a word
he's just translated. The Latin is so good and clean it shines
a halo around his head. What he wants is not to copy meaning
but explain. He'd rather be writing marginalia, but he won't.
All the marks he makes have a meaning like every object
in his room, his books, slippers, cushions, scissors—
all cut finely in the plate like iron filings drawn
into place by those meticulous fingers. He will stay
until his work is done. His dog curls up asleep.

How much of this is true? None of the light
through the windows, nor the windows (from early
Renaissance Italy), nor the fine wood timbers of the ceiling,
the carefully cut lines of new theories of perspective.
These Dürer etched to furnish the European mind—
the *vita contemplativa*, Jerome in his Study, though truly
curmudgeon, a worried soul, and, of course, brilliant.
Actually, he came from the Syrian desert to live
in Bethlehem in a lightless cave, adjacent to the cave
of the Nativity, where animals were born in hay.
His walls were black with smoky oil from the lamp
by which he worked. Almost everything is artificial, made up
in scratch, one translator of another. The skull's a nice touch.
Only the words and the work and the lion are true.

In a dark room of the British Museum, the picture
is lowlit behind glass. Dürer, Jerome—each
hunched over the page, the plate in its acid bath;
each bent into what he believes will bring him
closer to what he desires. Truth for Dürer,
a God, for Jerome. And for us? We don't know

who we are, unless: we look in
to inwardness itself, an odd light streaming
through bull's-eye glass, magnified and burning.
It's a holy text. The mind moves through it,
painstakingly apprehending a mind remote,
what we desire most: the intimacy of a room
where we lose who we are, the *via negativa,*
and ciphers fill with ink black as stars.

ROSES ON THE CEILING

The head of Keats that Severn
drew at three in the morning,
"to keep myself awake," brought
me to Rome and the room
where he died under a ceiling
of phony roses.

That sketch of a face on a pillow
and its shadow black on the wall—stark,
haunting even, though
the eyes are closed, his lashes
thick as a girl's. Some inky curls
figured on the forehead
are limp and matted wet with fever.
From the long deft line
of the nose, the pen never lifted.
The scrutiny of Severn is in it,
the exactness of his seeing,
all those nights and days
when nothing else was.

The first morning in Rome
I walked to Keats' house
the roundabout way he'd ridden
his rented horse through the big streets,
past the churches, up the hill
from Piazza del Popolo, where there's a view—
as much of Rome as he ever saw.

In small hours, to stay awake,
Severn rigged a thread from one candle
going out to the wick of another.
Keats, his wide eyes growing into death,

saw it sputter like a firefly and told
at morning of a little fairy lamplighter.

He called for more and more books,
though he read little, the smell
of his rotting lungs competing
with the smell of leather.
He practiced the new Italian
in his head and, studying the roses
on the ceiling, turned the Greek
sweet music of his mind
to warm pictures of daffodils
on Hampstead Heath, a patch of
English violets on his Roman grave.

We want to be changed
by what we enter, the dry,
bright air of warmer places
to which we book passage,
roads of emperors and poets strewn
with marble victories,
intimate rooms where the famous
dead lived vividly, where what
was beautiful was not easy
and what was true was almost endurable.

The room where Keats died
is smaller than I had supposed
and narrow and empty.
No bed, no chair, no candle, no book.
Only, on the wall, Severn's sketch,
about the size of a thumbprint,
and roses on the ceiling
blooming in squares, gaudy and gold.

MARBLE BOY
for Harriet Harper, 1937–2004

I wanted you to see the marble boy.
So I gave you directions, for the bus
from Florence to Fiesole, and a little trattoria
for lunch, and afterwards a walk I'd taken once
around the hilltop, and knew you'd like,
with a view of the Arno and the bridges.
It would be, we knew, your last trip.

In the museum, you took notes for me
and made a sketch of the boy's broken feet,
the long toes of the paw with its nails,
and the tail curling up in half relief,
rising then several inches abstract in air.
It wasn't a snake but the tail of the lion
snapped off, a jagged end of stone.

And that was all—just enough to know
he was Heracles, not the man but the boy.
He might have had a club in his hand,
the skin of a new-slain lion slung
over his shoulders. He might have pushed
his head through to the skull to peer out
the way we know a boy would do with a trophy.

So many things are made up in myth
and history. I should stick to what
you wrote: "right foot broken at ankle,
all toes intact, left foot broken above the ankle,
missing part of the big toe."
I would like to have seen the whole boy,
his chest, the muscles of his shoulders

modeled from the dark veiny seams
of the marble, and how strong or soft
the flesh of his hands, how much

the boy was already becoming the man.
Some miracles happened, we've been told,
at Nemea, the hero, smart and strong,
and able to endure almost anything.

It's strange, we agreed, he survived at all.
You sent me a postcard which I keep:
"I looked especially carefully at the feet."
I've stared and stared at the feet, and in the air
above the broken feet, and seeing nothing
but all that you endured, I've tried
in the empty light to see all that I've lost.

GREEK STONES

It looked like a graveyard, the hot, ill-lit room.
Stones stood upright, ancient *stele*.
Some boxes like small tombs, their lids thickly inscribed.
Every stone looked heavy, every surface pocked with decay,
layers like lace sloughing off.
I expected decorations, acanthus at least.
Nothing but Greek—letters archaic, lines
irregular, uneven, sloped, no pattern of spacing.

Kneading a dark stone as if it were flesh, as if
each incision, deep-sharp or shallow-worn,
were a knot of meaning loosening,
we learned to read distinctions with our fingers.

That afternoon the epigrapher
held up a white marble fragment like a small fetus
the size of a man's fist, shaped like the Greek letter
delta or, upside down, like the letter *rho*.
A round lump with a curling tail, it looked like a big white comma.
He began pointing at letters, then spelling:
Alpha Iota Sigma Xi—Aischylos, the name
fell from my mouth in the hollow museum.
He set the stone in my hands.

Dimly I saw the poet's tough heart,
a glint of his mind like an ax cutting down
through bone in the back of Agamemnon. The off-stage cry.
His voice in the mask of the furious woman.
Resonant, large. The altering pitch of wild singing.
Thudding meters of the choric dance.

—from a tablet set up in the *agora*, the epigrapher said,
a list of festival contest winners.
For what year—we don't know;
for poet or actor—we don't know.

At the end of the lesson, he put the stone back
in the case he locked with a key.

The next morning from storeroom crates of marble rubble,
we picked out fragments with inscriptions.
If we found one with a word we recognized,
or even part of a word, we considered ourselves lucky.
We learned to beat with a brush wet thick paper into the incisions.
The dry white documents we read like Braille, backwards.

In my fingers and my throat, the feeling
of *aoide*, the word for song, like wind
in the lyre, the sound of grieving;
and *aidos*, a word nearly impossible to know,
meaning something like honor or shame.
Some sense of refined morality we've lost,
some duration and pitch of the voice.

MAIANO

When Leonardo walked up into the hills of Fiesole
with his flying machines, he never ceased to study
the flight of birds, configurations of feathers and wings,
the physics of shouldering air. So that when the machines failed,
as they always did, crashing on stone terraces
of olive groves, splitting some of the oldest trees,
he still had new designs in his head, configuring and reconfiguring,
when he walked down again to his shop in Firenze.
That madman, that menace eluded authorities, the wrath
of the poor farmer whose daughter was hopelessly intrigued—
he knew that old dance, though he had the usual
preference for boys. He would shift ground, move around
a little south to the hill of Maiano,
where we eat lunch today on a leafy terrace.

You hear and see the birds in trees at the top of the cliff,
an excellent position for launching flying machines.
There is a view and the waiters are practically perfect,
attentive but leaving us be for a conversation
we are not having. I consider Leonardo
so that when my machinations fail to intrigue you,
as they inevitably do, I listen to the song of a bird,
a particular musical twitter as from branch
to branch it leaps, and savor a good Tuscan stew
and figure the seasoning, and flirt with the waiter who pours
lemoncello in two champagne flutes.
He downs a shot with us from your water glass.
Saluté. A bittersweet finish. Then
he kisses me twice on both cheeks, but not you.

CHRISTINE, DAUGHTER OF IMMIGRANTS
for her daughters, Carol and Lois

Before she dies, your mother tells you
of life in the black fields of Germany before she married
and came to this house and this room where she lies
seven years dying of pernicious anemia.

You see as she tells you the black fields of potatoes
like ugly stones stacked in piles and ready for battle,
her hands green with vines she has pulled
and calloused by the spade she leans into,

the edge of her long dress stained with mud
hot and stinking with rotting potatoes.
She tells you of days she fainted in the fields
and her father carried her a long way—

his boots sucking in and out of the mud,
the hem of her dress dragging—across rows
of potatoes to a cart of straw where he left her
unattended for hours in the sun with pain

like the labor of childbirth drawing her knees up
hard against the straw and no water for her throat
so dry with breathing through her mouth and the dark

red flow of her blood soaking through her dress
into the straw and the grain of the wood that she scrubbed
but never entirely cleaned of the stain.

THE MOTH

When she comes to bed on tiptoe, she's facing
the oil lamp on the nightstand. She's almost dreaming.
Her body knows the slow choreography of moving
toward sleep, even as the mind drifts. Nothing's there.
Already she's pulled the counterpane back from the corner,
just far enough to slip into the soft sheets,
rumpled folds like valleys and hills of a landscape
she knows and will again walk into, soon-to-be warm.
Over her arm a silk nightgown falls as thin
and easy as water. The cold floor is gleaming.
But who, you might ask, is the gazer, the painter
who looks and strokes? And what is she feeling?
Her body is lit flesh-rose, just fresh from bathing.
Her face in shadow, her hand is up against the light.

She's trying to see the moth. Is it death? Is it life?
Drawn to light, it is large, its sudden wings spread wide
like a specimen in a book, flat like a stencil on the wall,
an ugly tattoo she's seen on a man at the circus.
Is it real? Its double white wings repeat the pattern
in the counterpane, a child's red whirligig in a box of toys.
She'd just like to know what it means, though she's not
yet pulled from her dream of the painter, who looks at her
as he always looks at girls, the hint of breasts,
dream of the woman he can't be. There's a sadness
for you—this truth you look at: what you cannot be.
When she wakes wondering what it was,
where it went, her fingers will have touched
the dusty moth and kept some glitter from its wings.

THE BREAM

Breaking the living
film with my hand,
I touch the fish
no one has touched
or seen where he lived
nosing swiftly
through a forest
of reeds, at ease
on any dark level.
My cunning depends
on his intelligence,
on his own good need
changing in a silent
run the shape
of his mouth opening,
closing over my fat cricket
impaled, still wriggling,
now swallowed whole.
Cutting the last
surface, he has come
beyond his knowing,
swinging too free
in what he cannot
swim through, the panic
of air, desperately
believing the barbed
fin rising is made
for my hand.
The insistence of his long
bone, his full
strength focused,
is almost enough.
His back is as wide
as the reach of my hand.
For the sake of his mouth

I push the hook
back in his narrow
throat. He is shining
iridescent, blue.
His thin, red
gill breathes
the impossible air.
His round, perfect
eye sees
me, a shadow
in an old dream
of pure light.

KAYAKS

A kayak again. A double-ended paddle in my hands.
Blue Tahoe this time. A crisp light cool on silk.
The color and shimmer of a dress my mother once wore
to a dance with a man she wanted to marry.
Easy, currentless water near shore. Big boats far out.
We are looking at docks and brown-shingled
houses, and imagine views of the water
from kitchen windows, people together
in yet another variety of domestic life. A good life,
if people aren't quarreling and money doesn't run out.
I know you know what it's like. You would like this life.

I'm following your kayak along the shore.
The rise and dip of the paddle. Water slides
cold to my hands. I drift, farther out, drawn
by big space of nothing but water. Sun burns
a good heat, a good ache in my shoulders.
I don't feel much anymore.

Once I saw in dry dock: an axe had broken through
the bottom of a big pleasure boat, the blond wood perfect,
the varnish gleaming, except for the splintered hole,
a raw opening ripped into the ruined hull's pitch.
Envy? Rage? Self-loathing? What would it take?
The day of the axe.

Kauai, that time. Words in the morning, quietly—
you were sure. Language of tenderness
drained to thinness. A brutal act, unexpected.
The cancelled kiss. We didn't eat, didn't move
that long afternoon into evening.

I was looking at the sea from a window of the room
where we'd slept, how each wave sent up a wisp of spray

at the top of each muscular curl. A roiling surf.
Warnings we'd seen posted. Yet this delicacy thrown off.

The next day you might say was a miracle,
the hard work of just going on. A kayak,
a double kayak. Up the muddy river, a firm
but not impossible current, the forest steaming
green after the rain. All we could do was
paddle the river—the steady beating of heart work.
Tropical. It had stopped raining. Mud dribbled in rivulets,
bled red. The forest a tangle of black vines like thick arms
of a great water animal reaching down.
A long way in from the river, I kept slipping in the slick
clay muck, catching swinging vines, crawling
under, over. Couples on the trail wore expensive
boat shoes, new-gear shorts, designer shirts with big flowers,
birds painted on. Feet sucked in and out
of red mud. Someone with a ukulele was singing
about a little grass shack. The noise of it
thrumming the nerves. The slow trudge. The dripping
trees. The ruined shoes. The ugliness of it all
and the ache. Petals of plumeria scattered
on the wet ground, bruised, rust-blotched.

And then the waterfall and the rocks.
A loud loveliness unexpected, the tall light of it
washing out speech. I leaned on a rock
and watched you swim in the cold pool.

A kayak again. Blue Tahoe. Deep and so clean
I see green rocks on the bottom. Tomorrow
we'll hike the dry hills and look back,
the lake a lapis stone in a green wilderness.
We'll climb and circle down to the car,
a fine red dust hanging in alpine light,
the rare high air we breathe tingling
with the life we have. Here and now.
What we have come to.

PRETTY ROOMS

And if no piece of chronicle we prove,
We'll build in sonnets pretty rooms.

John Donne
"The Canonization"

1. THE MOWER

Saturday morning, the neighbor boy comes too early
for his money. The doorbell's rung. We wake remembering
the green bills ready on the table, the mower's pattern
in the grass, the swimming heat of yesterday's sun.
When night dew warms, humid air is not so heavy.
We're breathing as though we still slept, our bodies bent
toward each other. The flowered sheets we've pushed off.
Nothing's more comfortable than this.
Imagine the blonde boy on the doorstep, tightly wound
in his sneakers, trying to look cool through the peephole.
His mother is frying bacon; his father is shaving.
He figures we're in the shower, the kitchen radio's too loud.
Outside we know the grass smells fresh as laundry
from the dryer. Inside we begin to move again.

2. TRIO

Tonight I listen to Mozart measure his mind
across the harpsichord and then the flute sings,
a bird tipping the topmost bough, whistling
a sure note, the slow cello coming under like a warm wind
stroking the shining feathers at the throat,
shaking the lightest leaves of the silver maple.
All is transformed to pleasure and harmony,
endless and transmutable, a form compacted of the human mind
and heart. I imagine you at home far away from me,
listening to Mozart or the whistling of your kettle,
making tea, or stroking your thin cat, settling down
to your night's work: a lapful of student papers,
ciphers you put your mind to, seeking clarity
in a mind's fresh chaos, a flash of winter light in the tree.

3. ANNIVERSARY

Not knowing how we may spend our Saturday, I tinker early
in the garage, fitting a new tube around the rear rim
of my broken-down bike. Pumped up inside the tire,
it's tight and cuts in like a dull blade. Nothing's easy.
I want more than two hands but can do without, knowing where
yours are: one's holding the phone in the kitchen. You're talking
to someone I don't know, too long but very sincerely, she needs you.
The other's stroking the back of your best cat, limp in your lap,
she's almost sleeping. I ride out in a warm wind,
morning light cool on my hands, streaked with grease
from the chain. Cars speed by. With the jagged edge
of my key, I cut an armload of tall yellow flowers, blowing open,
balanced all the way home on my knees. Pumping faster
to come sooner, I'm hearing that voice again, envying her and her.

4. ROUSSEAU

Surrounded by museum glass, the white birches seldom
sway. The only motion's tiny green leaves budding,
and high up, frail as breath, the shedding tissue lifts.
So every tenderness growing faster splits noiselessly.
We could have found a bench in Central Park and talked.
That's what you wanted. I could walk no further, wanted
Rousseau's "Dream" again, a quiet place in the garden.
Pastels of one painting so unlike him, lilies larger than flamingos,
larger yet than figures darkly human—planes of life,
a grace of composition. Outside, reclining figure leans her head
in a pool of water. April's breeding. Moore and Matisse
conspire, faceless forms emerging rough-hewn from the wall.
Five slender trees rose up against the glass.
I imagined Monet's water lilies losing light.

5. AT NIGHT ON THE TERRACE, FIESOLE

Tonight I look out on the lights of Fiesole,
the shadow of the little campanile on the hilltop,
and the long dark line of trees along the Arno,
the winking lights of the bridges of Firenze,
and I know behind the slopes of Monte Ceceri,
big and red above the cluttered rooftops,
the Duomo of Santa Maria del Fiore
is certain and invisible. My mind goes there
remembering colors of stone pieced together
like quilt making, white and green and pink,
the dome's elegant marble ribbing, the scale
and feat of it, crying conceit and control.
Among things seen and unseen, how far can we know
what we know? How much can I tell you that is true?

Meanwhile the late Italian light has been taking
the last of the blood red roses on the terrace,
petals papery, perfume lost in the pungence
of magnolia and cypress, fig and rosemary.
High over it all, a half-moon rises while
across olives and vines now also in the dark,
the hollow clatter of the Fiesole bell clangs
hours and half-hours. The white dove we've seen,
tail fanning up, now settles and coos in the cypress.
Inside your slatted light of shutters you're in bed
reading a mystery—the whisper-turning of pages.
Drowsy in my arms on the table in the cooling night
of the terrace, I look out on the lights of Fiesole
and make no promises, not even to myself.

6. FOURTH OF JULY

Leaving the Esplanade after the fireworks
we follow paths along the dark glimmering river,
willow and water shadows wound with human figures.
Hot blankets and baskets, thermoses, folded umbrellas
slow-poking the night ground. Heat now bearable.
Red Line trains arrive above us at Charles Station:
window squares of lighted faces, heads like party
balloons loose on the ceiling, arms like hooks into meat.

On the lawn before Fiedler and the Pops, a young woman
in a white dress waited for her lover. She was reading
a book. When she lifted a knee, I saw she wore
nothing under . . .

                 At the foot of the ramp, we break through
metal barriers, up a stairway to the platform.
A red rear light follows us across the river.

7. THAT HAT

Merely because I left you on a cold first
of January and flew away South again,
to my life again—a tall man in a gold
party hat singing drunk in the seat beside me
Auld Lang Syne, his clothes smoke-rank
and sour with champagne, and as I rose
in a cold white cloud, the engines hurling me
into new time, new space, all I could see
on the window was your face at the gate
cold and small in your white fur hat,
my lips breathing the soft fur of your hat,
whispering how I loved you, how I'd always
love you, knowing even then, merely
because I left you, you would think I lied.

8. THE TURTLE

How much of your life can you live entirely under
public surfaces, not breathing mammal air,
the dry-as-dust smell of it, sterile as stone?
Beautiful swimmer, when you move there swift as a current,
your body's not heavy, that delicate wise head stretches out.
Dark, deep in the soft pond bottom, how well
do you bear the hard leisure of thought, the slow wait
for the song of a bird, the old public dangers?
Weak eyes blink slowly. Is light hostile or good?
You smell as I smell the dank sweet rot of wood.
The raw end of a log where you've climbed puts out
new green leaves in odd abundance. Colored and carved
and polished like treasure, you sun until you see me,
the yellow flash of that last left foot pushing.

9. CARAVAGGIO

for my godson, Cameron

Square in the middle of the painting of the Holy Family
the back of the angel with grey wings is feathered
like a dove's and softly folded. She's perfectly at home
and will stay a while. She's looking at Joseph who's holding
the score of her music which can be read over her shoulder.
Even I can read it and begin to hear beautiful music.
Joseph is content to be helpful, his goodness through and through.
And the donkey's wet eye is moving, looking at me.
Meanwhile to the right of the angel are Mary and her baby,
a real one who looks like my godson in Chicago.
He's moving like a baby, squirming, his fists fighting
the air, feet fleshy with fat. Mary is dealing.
I like them all enormously, like unmet friends.
They seem to admit strangers. I want to move in.

10. CONSCIENCE
I fear my conscience because it makes me lie.
                                    —Robert Lowell

Having gone mad once and found a therapist,
who held my hand, so to speak, and listened to my litany
of confusion, and with a word here and there
put a finger on my words, sentence, nerves
unregenerated, whipping out in all directions,
having come, hat in hand, a single nod a blessing,
and having risen from that plush, modern chair
with lies at last coherent, strung like beads and told,
I want, five years later to the day, I want
still to write letters, wire roses, and compose
extravagant telegrams, *mea culpa, mea culpa*, elaborate
articulation of a full confession, like Luther or Augustine.
Love, do not listen to me. I am trying
to improve my image of myself.

11. FIG

We will not be there when the figs ripen
on drooping branches under which we stooped
to go through the gate of our house above Fiesole.
In weeks they grew fully bulbous, hard and stiff,
as intensely green as the furry-fobbed leaves
bigger than our hands, casting shadows on the yellow
wall, the gleaming blond of the wooden door
where you fumbled in the double locks with the key.
We will not be there when figs ripen and fall,
though my mouth was ready like a bird's for something,
something warm, almost humanly warm like a cheek,
purple-black splitting red and sweet and soft.
Golden bees will come and hum and take off
the clammy sweetness that was almost ours.

THE RED COAT

LILIES

On the new-scrubbed, wet-black chalkboard,
Mrs. Altman printed *First Memory.*
Stories, she instructed, we must turn up in our minds
like stones, like lizards, like treasures in a pirate's cove.

Go back, she said, earlier and earlier. Find it. Can you?
Commands. Soft questions. This assignment like hypnosis.
The mind's a dark place, a tumbled up closet. I did what
she told me and kept my eyes shut. The taste of thumb.

But Eddie Middleton was giggling and kneeing my desk,
and Lindy Riley wore too much, too-sweet, like gardenias,
perfume I had to keep breathing. She was letting her head drop
all the way back, her long hair fell on my hands like a whisper

from a traveler, a rabbit in a long dark hole. The mind's so fast
falling and tumbling.
                     I'm trying to see over a shoulder,
maybe Dad's or Uncle Homer's. Whoever it is is patting my back
to hush me, but I *am* hushed, and I don't like the bouncing.

A blur of window with trees, a table, the picture over the mantle
in my grandmother's parlor. A picture of lilies. White and green paints
on pink-brown paper. The leaves. Stiff, artificial. Flowers flat on the wall.
They're not real, I'm knowing, the beginning of seeing the world.

In second grade, I made several sentences on lilies.
I was careful not to erase holes in the wide-lined paper.
That, to my teacher, was important. It wasn't easy.
I wanted to write hard and dark and permanent.

ON THROWING A FISH IN THE WELL

for my sister Jo and my Hudson Mill cousins

When she said she wouldn't cook it—
it was too little and too much trouble to heat up
the grease and too hot in the kitchen already—
we threw the fish we'd caught into the well
before we cut its head off or scaled or gutted it.
It was flopping around on the green willow twig
we'd run up through its lower lip, the crisp red
gills opening and closing, its watery black
eye still looking at us when it flipped
from my hand over the rim of the well.
Then we all climbed up on something,
me on a wobbly old grinding stone,
and looked down the round brick shaft
of moss and fern. Our eyes caught
on a stuck-out piece where I'd seen once
a big brown spotted bull frog,
a blown-up balloon at his throat,
bellowing and croaking his broken bass note.
The fish had entered cleanly and made
a little echoing "plop." The water mirror
wrinkled in the deep bottom, silhouettes
like cutwork scissored in a ring.
I could tell when I moved my head
which shadow I was and waved at myself.
The fish was gone for good.

Every day we slid the well lid back
to check for a white fish floating dead.
It never happened. We wondered if the cat
had got it. But how? Maybe—and this
was our secret—the fish had found a narrow
way through layered hard rock
to the cold spring that fed the well. Maybe
he'd get back to the creek a mile away

where we'd caught him. Maybe—
and this was our sin, because it was a wild
imagining, a kind of lie we got away with—
if we were lucky and good and kept fishing,
maybe we'd hook him again
on a good worm from the stables,
or a cricket trapped in our hands,
or a speck of white larva from a fresh
wasp nest knocked down from the barn.
Only this time, if we did catch him,
a fish that smart would be stronger
and bigger and give us the fight of our life.
And maybe this time, if it wasn't too hot,
if it wasn't August, she would cook him.

TWO AT THE DOCK

Father, you tell me of your mother
who's come down to the dock
and caught a small fish.
It's shining as she lifts it.
Its silver scales reflect the morning sun.
I see her small precise eyes winking,
the silhouette of her hair like mine
in waves and curls, the backs of her hands
old with splotches.
They move over the fins expertly,
detaching the hook from the open mouth.
Blood of the gill runs
under the nail of her thumb.

I do not forgive you that neglect:
thirty-two years lonely
in a cold house of high ceilings
and photographs of Southern men.
I hear the echo of her feet
on the bare floor of the parlor.
She walks loping like me on bent legs.
But today she has come down to the dock
to see you and has caught a small fish.
There is joy in her face which is
beautiful in the sun.

You watch all this from some distance,
mending your nets, planning your day.

GOAT SONG

The bleating goat stood on the rusted frame
of the iron bed under an olive tree,
a rusted chain around his neck, around
the tree and the legs of the bed, so tangled
he could barely turn his head. But he did and looked
at us, at the bus from which we looked.

I was thinking of the world's ancient places,
what remains, how it happens: his head down,
browsing all morning, occasional click of hoof,
shiver of hide flicking fly—motion like a planet
beginning to wobble in orbit, entropy
inevitable, residual effects of such a motion.
One crooked leg unsteady on the edge of the frame,
three stiff feet trembling on rusted springs.

It could just have happened. Not neglect,
I didn't think so—in the shade of the olive
a tub full of water and a chain so long
the goat had dragged a wide dirt circle clean.
At least there was shade and no heavy breathing
through his mouth, his tongue not hanging out.
A gray mud-matted beard dripped from his chin.
At least, I thought, he's alive.

Our bus rolled by the goat and the bed and the tree
and we didn't stop. We were on our way
to Ox-Belly Bay—sand all around in a circle of blue,
silver around lapis. We walked around and swam across.
A small bay with a narrow gap between tall cliffs.
Currents swirled around big rocks—turbulent
waters Odysseus might have sailed through.
He found a cunning way to pleasure and moved on.

That hero. But the goat. How he got up there
I'll never know. A good long chain.
Cheap labor for cleaning the olive grove.

The unusual complication of the bed frame.
A quaint picture of authentic Greek pastoral life,
the tangled raw difficulty of it.

As I walked easy in the cool bay water
and swam across and back again—I'm not a strong
swimmer, I think too much—the odd glimpse,
such scruff, what you'd never photograph—
I couldn't get my mind off the goat. The dumb goat.

I wanted to make a meaning for the goat:
Suffering is wisdom. Or *wisdom is suffering.*
Someone else's meaning. No god or grandeur here.
Just a goat. A dumb suffering goat.

That morning we'd explored a hilltop temple—
or what was left of it: blocks randomly strewn,
fluted drums, lintels, a massive architrave.
We'd read the elegant big geometry of stones
and traced the mallet's stroke.
On the altar stone, evidence of ancient fire.
In excavations of a pit nearby,
fragments of black bone.

I hadn't yet seen the goat on the bed frame.
I hadn't yet eaten goat.

Lunch in a taverna in a poor village.
Chatter of Greek. Chairs scraped the stone floor.
Across the dirt street a fresh goat hung
in the shop door. The head and feet still on,
skinned to pink-gray bloodless meat,
fine lines of young muscle, the ribs
splayed out to show he'd been gutted clean.
"Trag" on a bloody tag in Greek, wired
to the lowest foot, so many drachmas per kilo.

The trag we got was good, fat and seasoned
with garlic, mint, and something hot
that wasn't pepper and just the right

coarse sea-salt to complement the fat.
I was sweating quietly in my seat on the bus,
good meat of goat digesting in my stomach
when I saw the goat. He was bleating,
but not yet desperately, at the bus.

Trag-oidia. A goat song.
The clean-swept arc of an orchestral floor.
This place of suffering and song.

Nothing I knew could help me with what I saw.

THE RED COAT

It's sleeting when we walk from the white church,
the ground frozen, the brown grass brittle.
I am somewhat back in the long black line of mourners,

behind my sisters, their husbands and children. I see it
all as it's happening as though it's not happening.
The roses on the polished oak of my father's coffin

are sheeting with ice and I know the red coat
is too thin to keep my mother warm. She's not shivering.
She walks across the breaking grass behind the coffin

slowly and with great dignity—without her oxygen tank,
her mouth open, a rose filled with snow.
She's walking toward something silver and mechanical,

like a fence around the grave. There's a canopy imprinted
with the logo of the funeral home, *Herndon and Sons*,
and four rows of white plastic chairs and the artificial grass.

A blue tarp covers a red clay pile of earth. We aren't supposed
to notice these things. Bits of color in wool hats and scarves
and the red coat. My mother was determined to wear the red coat

which I'd bought for myself but gave to her because she loved it,
because it is the color that he loved on her,
because I could not bear her not having anything she loved.

ABOVE THE TOWN

Because she loved him, he wanted to take her flying
above the town. And so, there they are, big in the sky,
the rooftops of Vitebsk all below,
parallelograms in shades of green.

Just looking at them, odd like that,
so much exuberance in the curving lines,
it's impossible to know: how did they do it?
He of green earth, she of sky.
Paint thin as watercolors.

She floats, a swaddle of blue dress,
her shoes pointed, with a single strap,
modest, a little apart. His arm around her,
his hand at her breast. She's having
a fling, her hand out front in the sky,
as if she were Superman, as if
the man she married is following her lead.
He was in love with her all of her life.

His black boot, the darkest spot,
drops clumsily, his other foot is lost
in her dress. Their faces are blank,
dove-gray. But he's done it, has lifted the girl
he married in a Sunday sky.
We cannot go where they are.

Among the green houses below,
one in the center is red.
Windows are hatched like tic-tac-toe.
Fences are vertical shades
of black and gray, a wandering crinkle

of boards, each pointed with a sharp stroke.
A ladder leans up to a loft,
a miniature goat is browsing.

There are no people in the town except
a tiny old man on our side of the fence.
He's bent in that peculiar shape
of acrobats before the backward flip.
His pants are dropped. He's about to take a crap.
He's looking so hard at the ground,
he couldn't possibly notice what is filling the sky.

I look and look until
my mother's kitchen fills
with the sweet butter smell of a cake
she makes for my father,
until I hear the song he sings for her:
Ah sweet mystery of life . . .
The heart aches and aches,
and, because it must, grows wings.

THE MARSH

Wherever the great water rolls in
pulled by the moon
                over broad flat lands
you will find my father in August
casting his net at the sun,
at the moon, up the mouths of saltcreeks,
at the edges of marsh grasses
                      where shrimp run
just under shallow water.

In the South's hottest month, you learn to swim
like fish through air
              heavy with water.
Fishermen find a shade to mend their nets.
But the sun doesn't matter to my father,
who does as he pleases in August.
He sleeps by the moon,
                between tides,
six hours in, six hours out.
Neither he nor the ocean can be held longer
from the pull of the moon on the earth,
from whatever it is that draws him to his dock.

This is the land we came from,
half mud, half water, open to the sky.
The salt in our blood
                is the salt in this air.
Diving home we hear: the ocean still sings
like a shell
          one perfect note.
We were the sheephead, sly bait-taker
with rows of human teeth.
We were the crab
            crawling out of the tide,
heavy and awkward with armor,
sputtering a threat of water, raising a claw.

Our eyes on stalks, we saw
the distant islands of palmettos we came to.
This is the land my father shares with salt creatures,
each subject to the whim
                              of the moon,
the ravages of spring tides:
bluecrabs, stonecrabs, fiddlercrabs,
mullet and redfish and croakers,
flounders and flats of oysters,
and the rolling schools of blue porpoises.

But the mysterious creekshrimp is his god,
no bigger than his thumb. The transparent head
breathes water,
                        pulsing the length of his back.
The double flip of the tail lets him run
faster than fish, the long needle horn of his head
jabs painfully
                        whatever arrogantly holds him.

Over a cold night in November they vanish
to the colder sea.

But in August, they run with the tides,
filling saltcreeks from the rivers,
                              feeding at the edges
of grasses where the white crane waits,
regal and motionless near my father,
poised above water,
                        steady on the bow
of his boat. The rhythm of his back
is the rhythm of the moon
                              pulling the sea out
and letting it go,
turning his net out in one motion,
letting the cords slip from his teeth
                                        through the bone-white
horn of his net, opening above water so easily,
so lightly
            the shrimp do not know to leap

until caught, pushing the mesh out
alive and growing heavy with water.

In August, in the humid salt air of the night
or the heat of noon, my father knows
the sun going down or rising
                              is red
over the eastmarsh, over the westmarsh.

THE GLIDER
for my sister, Lynn

There's no reason for her to have bopped me
on the head with the hard rubber end of her silver
twirling baton, except that I didn't want to play majorette
and so she wasn't fair and I know I wasn't either,
though I tried as my father told me to walk in her shoes.
But those shoes? Must I have walked, pranced around
in those shoes? My sister is five years old
in the photograph and I'm seven.

I don't know what my mother intended
sealing us up like this in the aftermath of the quarrel.
She'd come out of the house with the Kodak.
Don't you dare move, she said to my sister.
Hush your crying, she said to me with no pity,
and put us side-by-side on the porch glider with its red
plastic cushions, their big painted-on flowers.
The knot on my head swelling and throbbing.

My sister is grinning big in the photograph,
the scuffed-up soles of her shoes sticking straight out
at the camera, and I'm serious, my eyes
black pools into which the world has dropped
its hard and simple questions. She's stepping high in the grass
pretending she has white boots on—little pom-poms swishing,
her baton flashing, the whole football stadium
screaming for more of her fancy foot-and-wristwork.

Fifty years later, we're looking through tins of loose
family photographs and here it is in black-and-white,
the cushions gray now, the flowers
white camellias—we'd forgotten that part.
But we both remember her time-out on the glider,
the worst kind of punishment, especially for her.
She's not pouting, she's fidgeting and plotting
an early escape, the glider bumping and squeaking.

I'm looking at the photograph—yes, it was right there
it all began, discovering and settling our differences—
I sat on the brick steps with my chin in my hands
and studied the green summer grass. And night after night,
Dad came out after supper and sat between us. We played
count-the-cars until dark and headlights came on
and we couldn't any longer see the models of the cars
and we counted the stars to the end of the numbers.

Mother is gone now and father too,
under the grass, settled together just months ago.
We're tearing apart the house we lived in,
everything trashed or boxed-up, clothes in plastic bags,
furniture collected for the Salvation Army. Everything's
a mess, an impossibly organized arrangement
of drolleries with a merciless logic. My sister tells me
what to do—to sort things out and let them go.

Pollock made this on the floor of his barn,
a bucket of house paint in his hand, his back bent
like the man in "The Man with the Blue Guitar."
Pure labor and attention as he walked the edges,
sweat and cigarettes and dogged intensity,
he heard the music in his mind.

The ground's a kind of half-tone, beige-gray.
Splatters blue-green and blurred washes
and white streaks of thin line curling back
on itself, and black lines running everywhere
over the surface, like layers and tangles of a bird's
nest or convolutions of the human brain,
its neurons and synapses.

Nodes of meaning dribbled with trowel and stick.
A track quick like a bird chased in a square.
It moves and doesn't know where to move.
Or stops still. Snail glisten on dry ground.
The story is that there is no story, just the ache
and meaningless grace of the body, a dance
that has vanished. The painting only itself.

Close up, I count the threads of raw canvas.
The museum clicks and hums like machinery.
I could say: In the garden, Picasso's goat has snow on his back.
I could say: Magritte's blank faces cannot kiss.

I could say. But I have no story to tell.

A man made this picture the year I was born.

ON A BUS TO THE AIRPORT, COLORADO

The window is filling with snow,
and then completely is gone
blank as Locke's slate,
a mind rubbed clean with a cold
washing of snow. Nothing's there.
This happens slowly
so that what I see is gradually

less than what I hear, the whoosh,
whoosh of the wide blades cutting an arc
across the world, thin ice shaving off,
the hiss of sleet hitting glass,
and tires beginning to crunch
the black ice, the rough ice, the dirty ice
thrown up like trash along the road.

Inside the warm bus, among quiet strangers,
I see in the white blur only the thinnest lines
of a wire fence, the blip, blip of gray posts,
for miles the same fence, a score
without notes—long, silent, equal measures.
Only in the West could this happen—
thousands of acres of fenced-in snow.

A big faint winter tree in a field of white.
Then, the outline of a barn, as if etched
by young Dürer directly on the plate.
And here, a window in a peaked roof,
like a birdhouse I hung in summer once
from a green limb. I watched from my window
little birds huddle in the near dark.

Can we unknow what we know? For there:
"a feverish huddle of shivering cows,"
as Lowell saw them, hundreds in vague clumps
like tufts of grass across a milky field,

their bony backs collecting snow.
They just stand there, noses together
breathing each other's air.

Closer to the congestion of the city,
highway equipment: yellow and green
and orange caterpillar bulldozers crusted
with snow. Toys abandoned in a sandbox.
Crayons scattered in a ditch, lopsided,
dribbled with snow. A fauve geometry
on the graded slope. Nothing's constructed now.

It's wonderful to see the snow,
how it edits and rephrases, and builds up
obliterations and makes fresh again,
makes cold and still again, and in the plain,
uncluttered mind, muffles the living and the dead,
those I'm coming from, those I'm going to,
those I love, those I don't want to think about anymore.

Epilogue

FACE

The bleeding head looked up from the black road,
A white shirt on the shoulder and the arm pushing up,
The asphalt gritty and black, the white staccato
Streaks of speed. An accident. I was driving east
In a black night toward the coast on a map, toward love.
Warm, I hoped, at the end of the road. Late
And so few cars on the wide, divided highway.
Fear of drift. Taste of salt. Sound of speed.
And then the headbeams of my car caught the face,
White like the shirt. Hair on the brow a lick of blood.
My car swerved to miss the bleeding face
In the road. Then I woke up. I knew who he was.

My father's brother, killed at the age of twelve
In a hunting accident, years before I was born,
Years before my father knew my mother.
They were taking guns out of the back floor
Of the car, doves still bleeding, fluttering in the sack,
And a gun his cousin lifted, loaded, his finger
On the trigger, carelessly. He didn't know what
He was doing. And my grandmother ran toward the shot,
Ran and ran at the sound of the shot—she couldn't know
What had happened. But she knew. Younger then
Than I am now, she got over it, and was kind.
There was no enduring sadness in her.

I admired how she killed a rat in her kitchen
With a flyswatter once, how she watered flowers
On her porch and they bloomed and bloomed.
She lived forty more years in the big house
With a gun under her pillow, his photograph
A large oval over the mantel in the living room.
Old women, great aunts, smelling sour
Like old flesh, sweet powder and mildew,
Would grab me, feel my bones, said I looked
Just like him—that I was a girl didn't matter—
The small mouth, the cheekbones. I used to
Stare at his handsome beauty—the dark eyes.

What the mind does for the mind should be a kind
Of healing, and maybe this is. I had forgotten
How their hands moved over me until the dream
Of the young man dying in the road, whom cars ignored
As I did, speeding toward love week after week
And never arriving—the oddly familiar boy,
The bleeding face looking up from the road,
The head without a body, none that I could see,
The mangled car in the dark burning up.
I didn't get a good look. It doesn't matter
How it happened, who abandoned the scene,
Just that he's bleeding. I did nothing but swerve.

I wake to birds in trees on another coast.
Nobody lives here that I know. Week after week,
I sleep dreamless. And I have made a pact
With desire. Affections sustain me. A quiet hour
With an open book and a dear face near me in the dark.
I wake to redwoods, firs, and a view over islands
North into Canada, a distant ridge of mountains
Rimmed with snow, and this comfortable oddness
Of feeling him sometimes alive in my shoulders,
In the way I hold my hand on my knee, as if waiting
In the woods with a gun in my arms, quietly searching
The white sky, the bare autumn trees for birds.

NOTES

The French Bed. After the etching (1646) by Rembrandt, which I saw at a Rembrandt exhibition, The Art Institute, Chicago, March 2004.

Fugitive Effects. Six of Monet's *Haystacks* are hung side-by-side on a single wall in the Chicago Art Institute. Monet wrote: "The only merit I have is to have painted directly from nature with the aim of conveying my impressions in front of the most fugitive effects."

Marsyas. Anish Kapoor's gigantic sculpture *Marsyas* (2002), composed of three steel rings joined together by a single span of PVC membrane, filled the Turbine Hall of the Tate Modern. Two rings were positioned vertically, at each end of the space, while a third was suspended parallel with the bridge. It was designed to look like bleeding flesh. Reference in the poem is also made to the portrait of Iris Murdoch (1984–1986) by Tom Phillips in London's National Portrait Gallery; painted in the background of that portrait is Titian's *The Flaying of Marsyas* (1575–76). I saw the installation in January 2003.

Front Page New York Times. I am grateful to the photojournalists and photo editors of the *New York Times* and other wire services whose photos are the subjects of these poems. I am also grateful to the journalists who reported the Israel-Lebanon war in the summer of 2006. I was prompted to respond to these photographs by a comment made by Eleanor Wilner, that we as poets have some obligation to be political. Early in the drafting of these poems, Carol Frost gave valuable advice.

Dürer's Jerome. After the etching (1514), which I saw at a Dürer exhibition, The British Museum, January 2003.

Marble Boy. The marble base fragment (Roman replica of Greek original second century B.C.) is in the Archeological Museum, Fiesole, Italy.

Greek Stones. The Epigraphical Museum in Athens is the setting of this poem. The scholar who attempted to teach me to read inscriptions on stones is David Jordan. Aeschylus, who wrote the fifth-century B.C. Greek tragedy *Agamemnon*, may have played the role of Clytemnestra himself, his voice in her mask.

The Moth. After the painting (1959) by Balthus.

Rousseau. Art works referred to include: Henri Rousseau's "Dream" (1910), "The Flamingos" (1907); Henry Moore's "Family Group" (1948–1949); Henri

Matisse's series "The Back (I-IV)" (1908–1931); Aristide Maillol's "The River (1943); and Claude Monet's "Water Lilies" (c. 1920).

Caravaggio. After his painting "Rest during the Flight into Egypt" (1595), Galleria Doria Pamphilj, Rome.

Goat Song. I saw the goat who is the subject of this poem when I was a student at the American School of Classical Studies in Athens, Greece in the summer of 1991. John Fischer was my indefatigable teacher and guide.

Above the Town. After the painting by Marc Chagall (1914–1918), The Tretyakov Gallery, Moscow. In the Chagall Retrospective, San Francisco Museum of Modern Art, Summer 2003.

No. 1. After Jackson Pollock's *No. 1* (1948), Museum of Modern Art (New York) with reference to Picasso's *She-Goat* (1950) and to René Magritte's *The Lovers* (1928).

Idris Anderson was born in Charleston, South Carolina. She moved to the San Francisco Bay Area in 1991, when she won a National Endowment for the Humanities Teacher-Scholar grant which she held in the Classics Department at Stanford University. She has been the recipient of other NEH grants to study lyric poetry at Harvard University, Greek and Greek tragedy at Stanford, and Virginia Woolf in London.

She has published poems in *The Hudson Review, The Nation, Ontario Review, The Paris Review,* and other journals. She has been nominated for a Pushcart Prize for 2007. Her sequence of lyrics "Starfish at Pescadero" was set to music by composer Dennis Tobenski and premiered in Brooklyn, New York in November 2007, with Melissa Fogarty, soprano, and the contemporary chamber music group Percussia.

She has a BA from Columbia College, a PhD in Shakespeare from the University of South Carolina, and an MFA from Warren Wilson College's Program for Writers.

She is head of the Department of English at Crystal Springs Uplands School in Hillsborough, California.

Mrs. Ramsay's Knee is her first book of poems.

THE MAY SWENSON
POETRY AWARD

This annual competition, named for May Swenson, honors her as one of America's most provocative and vital poets. In the words of John Hollander, she was "one of our few unquestionably major poets." During her long career, May was loved and praised by writers from virtually every major school of poetry. She left a legacy of nearly fifty years of writing when she died in 1989.

May Swenson lived most of her adult life in New York City, the center of American poetry writing and publishing in her day. But she is buried in Logan, Utah, her birthplace and hometown.